The Cave of Reconciliation

by Pecki Sherman Witonsky

Acknowledgments

The author is grateful to Katie Scott, whose artwork alone can tell the story.
To Joseph Painter, photographer.
Studio West for the layout and design.
To the staff and students of The Hussian School of Art for artistic insights.
To The Shefa Fund, who sponsored the start-up process for this book.
To Jeanne Ayesha Lauenborg who first introduced me to
the Islamic story and the Dances of Universal Peace.
To Sharmin Achmed for inviting me into her community.
And especially to Carl who married me 45 years ago.

There are many others, people of faith, whose hope for a
better world encouraged, nudged and embraced this effort.
But, I take full responsibility for this retelling of Abraham's stories.

MAY THIS SMALL BOOK BE A GIFT IN THE SERVICE OF HEALING AND PEACE.

To order copies please contact:

DIAMOND ROCK PRESS
P.O. BOX 765
BRYN MAWR, PA 19010
www.caveofabraham.com
e-mail contact@caveofabraham.com

Genealogy

ADAM~m~EVE
↓
NOAH~
↓
TERAH~
↓
SARAH ← ABRAHIM → HAGAR
1800 BCE
↓ ↓
ISAAC~m~REBECCA ISHMAEL~
↓ ↓
JACOB   ESAU 12 SONS
↓
12 SONS
↓ QURAYSH TRIBE
DAVID
↓
JESUS
0–33CE

MUHAMMAD
570–632 CE

This is My covenant with you. You shall be the
father of a multitude of nations.

GENESIS 17:4

෧ᴍᴍ෧

The book of the genealogy of Jesus Christ, the son of David,
the son of Abraham.

MATTHEW 1

෧ᴍᴍ෧

Say, we believe in God, in what has been revealed to us
and what was revealed to Abraham, Ismail, and in the Books given
to Moses, Jesus, and the Prophets from their Sustainer. We make no
distinction between one and another.

SURA 2:136

෧ᴍᴍ෧

These and these are the words of the living God.

TALMUD

ABOUT 1800 B.C.E.

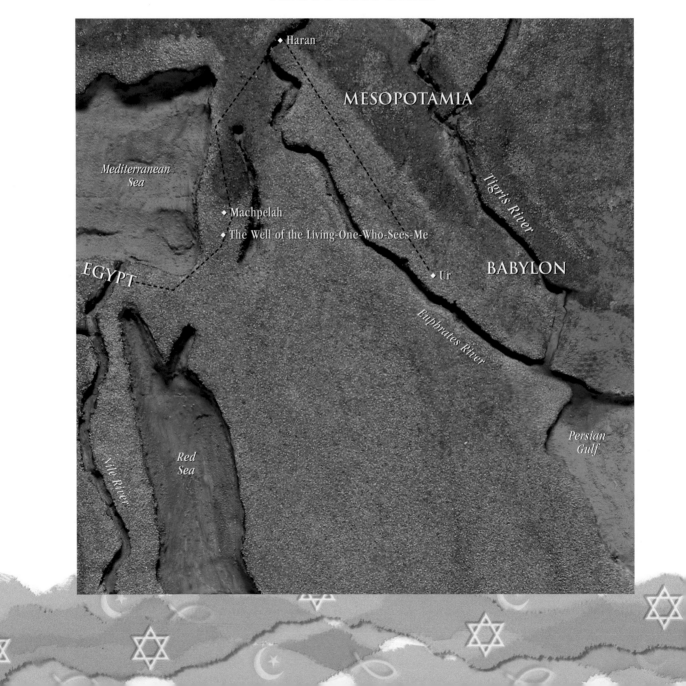

These are stories about Abraham. Stories of Abraham's deep faith in the God of Creation. Stories of his relationship with his two sons, Ishmael and Isaac, and their mothers, Hagar and Sarah.

These tales are ancient. They have been told by Jews, Christians and Muslims for generations — among families, as they sat around campfires and wellsprings in the deserts long ago. Today, people of all three faiths continue to recount the stories in their holy places, in their homes and even in films.

At different times in history, depending on the teller, events and locations change. For example, in the Judeo-Christian account, Isaac is offered up, while it is Ishmael who is brought forth for sacrifice in the Islamic story. Regardless of the version, the inspiration is Abraham's willingness to follow the voice of God. In each story, God's life-giving underground waters spout up in deserts, separated by hundreds of miles, at different times. Whatever the time or the location, in all versions, God is the source, the Aquifer, for all people of faith.

Whether Jewish, Christian or Muslim, at the heart of each telling is Abraham. Never faltering is the deep relationship between God and Abraham, and God, Abraham and all people of faith.

Here, we retell stories combining what we have heard with what has been written in the Bible. If you turn this book around and start at the other side you will be able to read the stories of Ibrahim as retold in the Islamic tradition.

As Jews, Christians and Muslims, we are all descendents of Abraham, the father of our faiths. The father whose sons came together peacefully to bury him in the Cave of Machpelah. *A place whose destiny is reconciliation.* The time has come for us to respect each other's faith in the One God, The Creator.

Shema Yisrael Adoni Eloheynu, Adonai Echad
Hear, O Israel, The Lord Our God, The Lord is One

bram heard a Voice – the Voice of the Creator, the One God filling his whole being with warmth and love. The Voice said, *Lech Lecha – Go forth to a land that I will show you, I will make you a great nation, you will be a blessing*. GENESIS 21:2

Now another man might have been entirely perplexed. After all, Abram was 75 years old and he and his wife Sarai were childless. But he realized that the Voice was the One he had been preparing for, and waiting to hear, his whole life. He knew it was the One Voice to trust and follow. He believed that with the help of the Voice, the One God, that he and Sarai could indeed start a great nation. As for his age, Abram's father Terah was 70 when he was born, and Terah lived 205 years.

Again, and yet again, The Voice repeated *Lech Lecha*. Abram knew this didn't just mean *go forth* in the physical sense. It meant *go forth and go deeply within your heart*. It meant that Abram was to follow the Voice with every ounce of his being, led and strengthened by a faith known by no other man. Somehow Abram knew that if he obeyed this awe-inspiring Voice, he would embark on a journey that would change the world forever.

Abram had known God since his early childhood.
He remembered an incident…

bram's father, Terah, made statues of gods. Today we call them "idols." These idols represented the different regional gods. Terah crafted these statues for the people of Babylon and their king, Nimrod, who considered himself to be a god-king. The people prayed to Nimrod and the idols.

As a little boy, Abram played in his father's shop among the statues. One day when he was alone in the shop, Abram took a stick and smashed the idols. Then he put the stick in the hand of the largest statue.

When Terah saw the mess in the shop, he was enraged. "What happened?" he demanded. Pointing at the large statue, Abram said, "He did it!"
Terah responded, "That's impossible, these idols are not alive, they have no breath!"
"Then why do people pray to them?" asked Abram.

Terah had no answer.

5

As Abram grew into manhood, he told people his idea of the One God, the God of Creation. Nimrod was beginning to worry about the effect Abram's stories had on the people. He decided to stop him. Nimrod had his slaves build a brick furnace filled with wood and ordered that Abram be tied and placed inside. Nimrod himself started the fire to show the people he was the most powerful god-king.

God, the God of Creation, sent an angel down to protect Abram. Days later, when the slaves opened the grate to the furnace, Abram walked out.

Nimrod never spoke of Abram or his God again.

So when Abram heard the Voice of God, he was ready to follow. After all, he already questioned the idols and was saved from the furnace by an angel of God.

Lech Lecha, go forth and go within.

Leave where you are living,

your father's family house.

Go to a place that I will show you.

There I will make you a great nation.

GENESIS 12:1-2.

When Abram's wife, Sarai, saw the light in Abram's eyes, she knew at once that it was time for them to leave their home in Haran. Still childless and advanced in years, Sarai did not understand how they could fulfill the "great nation" part of the promise. But as a devoted wife and faithful servant of God, she joined her husband willingly. She and Abram believed that if they kept faith in God, blessings would follow.

Sarai had the servants and slaves pack all their belongings while Abram and his chief steward Eliezer rounded up their flocks of animals. Together this small Abrahamic clan departed from the rich, fertile land between the two rivers. They began their journey to a place where the living-waters would go underground to reappear in wells and cisterns.

Those faithful first steps thousands of years ago were the beginnings of a nation built to serve the One God. To this day those first steps still connect all believers in the One God.

bram and Sarai journeyed to Shechem, where they found shade among the great trees. There, Abram built an altar and dedicated it to God. Then they rested and watered their flocks. Abram's step was light and confident, and Sarai was more beautiful than ever. Energized, they migrated south.

In time, Abram and Sarai began to face great challenges. In the desert they experienced a drought so severe that Abram needed to move his tribe into Egypt.

At that time, Egypt was ruled by a Pharaoh, a man who proclaimed himself to be not only king, but also god of Egypt. Pharaoh's guards were responsible for reporting all that went on in Egypt. They told Pharaoh that a new tribe had crossed onto his land and, that among the people, there was a woman of exceptional beauty. The woman was Sarai.

Pharaoh visited the tribe of Abram, and when he saw Sarai, he wanted her for himself. Now Sarai and Abram knew that it was illegal for a man – even a Pharaoh – to steal another man's wife. They both knew Pharaoh could order Abram's death, then claim Sarai as his own. In order to save his own life, an anguished Abram had Sarai pose as his sister.

Sarai was taken into Pharaoh's harem.

Pharaoh was intrigued by Abram and spent time talking to him about worldly and godly matters. So pleased was Pharaoh with both "brother" and "sister," that he gave Abram gifts of gold, silver, cattle and slaves. Among these gifts was a slave named Hagar.

Sarai could not bear serving Pharaoh and she prayed to God for help.
Seeing her anguish, God sent a plague on Pharaoh's house. When Pharaoh
realized that he had been tricked, and that the God of Abram had the power to
bring a plague on his house, Pharaoh returned Sarai to Abram and ordered them
to leave Egypt.

Fearing Abram's God, Pharaoh did not even take back the gifts.

When they left Egypt, Abram gave Hagar to Sarai.

bram and Sarai were faithful to each other as husband and wife. Abram could have taken other wives, which was commonplace at the time, but he chose not to. He and Sarai were best friends and confidants; together they had agreed to follow God's voice when He instructed Abram to *go forth to a place that I will show you.*

Though they had no children of their own, Abram and Sarai were recognized and respected as patriarch and matriarch of a large and growing clan. Over the years, everyone knew of the couple's faithfulness to God and their kindness to all their people – those who were free as well as those who were servants and slaves.

As Sarai aged, she remained a great beauty. But her hopes of having a child had passed. How could she help Abram fulfill the promise that God had made to him early in their journey, in Shechem, at the great trees of Morah? There, God had told him, *this land will belong to your children and your children's children's children forever.* Genesis 12:7.

Abram and Sarai discussed the possibility of adopting Eliezer, Abram's chief assistant. As their adopted son, Eliezer would inherit Abram's tribe and name.

Sarai liked Eliezer, but she knew that adopting him would not fulfill God's promise. Abram asked God for advice. God told Abram, *Only through your very own seed will you have an heir. Look up and count the stars, your descendants will number more than the stars*. GENESIS 15:4-5

Sarai knew of Abram's conversation with God. Desperate to help, she realized that there was one way for her to help Abram. She would give one of her slaves to her husband to bear a child. The child would belong to Sarai and Abram. In the ultimate act of generosity, *Sarai gave Hagar, her young Egyptian slave, to Abram as wife*. GENESIS 16:3.

Imagine how Hagar must have felt about bearing Abram's child. Having attended Sarai since they left Egypt, Hagar knew Sarai was barren. The laws of the time gave Sarai the right to use Hagar as a surrogate.

Hagar knew that if she had a son he would be a free man. He would be Abram's first born and inherit the leadership of the tribe. Hagar knew Abram and Sarai to be kind people, whose good reputations went far beyond the tribe.

Hagar went into Abram's tent that one night – nervous, but filled with hope for the future.

The next morning Hagar went back to serving Sarai. Six weeks later Hagar and Sarai realized Hagar was pregnant with Abram's child.

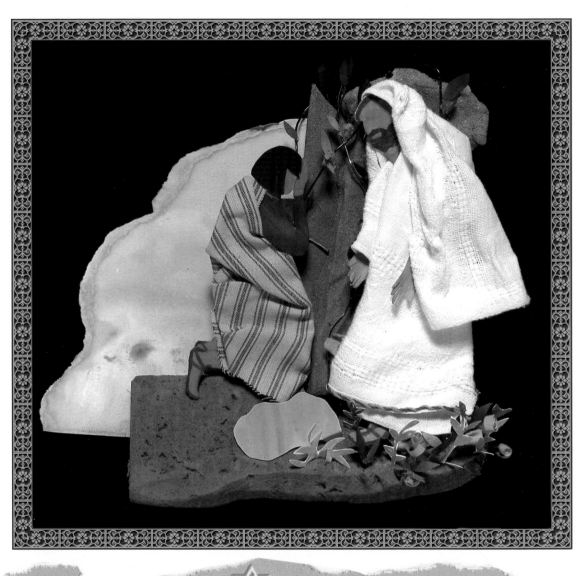

As the months passed and Hagar's belly grew larger, she became filled with self-importance. Hagar no longer wanted to serve Sarai or take orders from her. Both women were agitated, and they quarreled frequently.

Scared and desperate, Hagar ran away into the wilderness.

When she thought she could no longer survive, God sent an angel to her. At first, frightened, distressed and parched with thirst, Hagar did not see the angel standing before her. The angel asked, *Hagar, where did you come from, and where are you going?* Hagar managed to tell her story. The angel showed Hagar a bubbling wellspring from the aquifer that God provided for her. As Hagar drank from the well, she looked deeply at her own reflection. She realized that Abram's God had seen her, and she named the well, *Be'er l'chai roi.*

The *Well of The Living-One-Who- Sees-Me.* Genesis 16:13.

The angel told Hagar of God's promise – she would have a son, his name would be Ishmael, and he would father a great nation. The angel told Hagar to return to Sarai and Abram.

At the end of nine months, Hagar gave birth to a son. As God's angel had foretold, Abram named him Ishmael, *God Hears*.

Sarai never seemed to bond with Ishmael, so she left him in Hagar's care.

ears passed, then God appeared to Abram again. Abram bowed low to the ground. God said, *I am making a covenant with you. You shall be the father of a multitude of nations. Your new name will be Abraham. You will walk with me and I will always be in your thoughts and actions. This covenant will last forever. Every male in your tribe shall be circumcised. Sarai, your wife, will be called Sarah. She is blessed and will have your son a year from now.* GENESIS 17:1-16.

Abraham fell to the ground laughing in gratitude. He followed God's directions and circumcised every male in his tribe. At that time, Abraham was 99 and Ishmael was 13.

A few days after the ritual of circumcision, in the heat of the mid-afternoon sun, Abraham was resting in his tent. The flaps were up so that he could see in all directions. He saw three men approaching and ran to greet them. He gave them water to drink and washed their feet. Abraham would have been hospitable to any visitors, as was the custom in the desert, but there was something very special about these three. He asked Sarah to bake bread, then he selected his best goat for roasting.

From the tent, Sarah heard her name mentioned, and then heard the men say that she would bear Abraham a child in one year. She laughed at the idea. After all, she was 90 years old, and well past the childbearing age.

Despite her disbelief, God indeed had a plan for Sarah — a plan that would change her world and, bring her great joy. Just as God predicted, Sarah conceived Abraham's child. Abraham was one hundred years old when their son was born. They named him Isaac, meaning laughter.

On the eighth day Abraham circumcised Isaac.

Isaac brought laughter, joy and the promise of a new future into Abraham and Sarah's lives.

Some 2000 years later The New Testament records *the circumcision of Jesus on the eigth day, and the mother's (Mary) ritual purification in accordance with the Jewish law:* The Gospel of Luke 1:21-22.

hen Sarah stopped nursing Isaac, Abraham made a great party to honor the occasion. At the party, Sarah thought Ishmael was laughing and mocking the celebration. Because Sarah was concerned for Isaac's future, she did not want him to be influenced by his half-brother's wild streak. She was so upset, that she ordered Hagar and Ishmael be sent away. As matriarch of Abraham's tribe, Sarah used her authority to protect the birth-right of her son.

Abraham was distressed and did not want to send them away. God intervened and told Abraham to *listen to his wife.* The people who later would be called Jews would grow through the lineage of Abraham, Sarah and Isaac. God also told Abraham, *Ishmael would be a great nation.* GENESIS. 21:13.

The next morning, with a heavy heart, Abraham gave Hagar water and bread and sent Ishmael and her away. In his despair, Abraham did not remind Hagar of God's promise to Ishmael. Nor did Hagar remember how, the angel of God had once provided her with life-saving waters.

When their meager supplies ran out, Hagar panicked. She was afraid her son would die.

But God had not forgotten His promise. He heard Hagar and Ishmael's fear and sent an angel to them. Hagar dried her eyes. She saw water spouting up from the ground. The angel reminded her of God's promise. *Ishmael would be known as a great bowman he would father a great nation.* GENESIS. 21:19.

Hagar and Ishmael moved to Paran, near Egypt. There Hagar was comforted and free. *Ishmael became a great bow-man, and Hagar found him an Egyptian wife.* GENESIS. 21:21.

braham, Sarah and Isaac lived quietly and contentedly near Be'er L'chai Roi. At the well Isaac always felt God's presence.

Several years passed; then one day God called Abraham. He answered,

Here I Am.

God commanded, *take Isaac, to the land of Moriah, (the land of the Seeing) and offer him to me.* GENESIS 22:2.

Despite his grief at the very thought of this request, Abraham's faith in God was so strong that he responded to God's command without a question. He did not confer with Sarah, for he knew she would try to prevent them from leaving. Although child sacrifice was common in other tribes at the time, it had never been practiced in Abraham's clan.

With a heavy heart and a heavy step, Abraham took Isaac, two servants and a donkey, and they set out for the land of Moriah. Once out of Sarah's sight, Abraham collected wood for the eventual sacrifice.

On the third day, Abraham looked up and saw the place where God directed him. He ordered his servants, *wait for us here. The boy and I will go up to the mountain to pray to God, and we will return.* Genesis 22:5. Abraham's heart was ripped in half. He would never disobey God's command, but did he really have the strength to kill his beloved son?

Abraham placed the wood on Isaac's back, and together they trudged up to the top of the mountain. On the way up, Isaac, who was dragging behind, called to his father. A weary Abraham answered,

Here I Am.

Isaac questioned, *We have the wood, but where is the animal that we will sacrifice?* Genesis 22:7 Abraham could not look at his son when he replied, *God, will provide, my son. God will provide.*

Isaac fell silent and asked no more questions. Like his parents, Isaac had great faith in God. God was ever present in their lives and was thanked daily for his many gifts. Together, faithful father and son lumbered up the mountain.

When they reached the top, Abraham built the altar and placed the wood on it. Dutifully, yet sorrowfully, he bound a numb and compliant Isaac to the wood. Abraham took up his knife, closed his eyes and prepared to slay his son.

Before Abraham could bring his knife down, an angel of God called to him. *Abraham!* Abraham was so fearfully focused on the slaying of his son that he did not hear or see the angel and had to be called again, *Abraham!* Abraham heard the angel and answered once more,

Here I Am.

The angel grabbed his hand in mid-air and lowered it away from Isaac. Abraham managed to open his eyes. Relieved and stunned, he turned his anguished face away from his son and saw a ram struggling in the bushes. Abraham released Isaac, and placed the ram on the altar.

The angel of God called Abraham again, saying, *Because you listened to God, and showed such great faith and were willing to sacrifice your son, God will bless you. Your descendents will be as many as the stars of heaven and the sands of the shores. All the nations of the earth will be blessed through your descendents, because you did as God asked.* Genesis 22:15-18.

This story is told twice in the Jewish calendar year. In the month of Tishri on the second day of Rosh Hashana (the Jewish New Year) and again about five weeks later in the month of Cheshvan. In our English calendar this is usually in the month of September.

When the followers of Abraham learned what happened, they knew that child sacrifice would never be practiced in their nation.

Sarah felt her heart break when she learned about the near-slaying of her beloved son. After that, Sarah did not want to let Isaac out of her sight. She wanted to know where he was at all times.

And so it happened that when Sarah was one hundred and twenty-seven years, her heart finally gave out and she died.

Abraham was devastated by Sarah's death. She was his beloved wife, his partner in building a nation, the matriarch of their people, and the mother of his son, Isaac. To honor her life, Abraham wanted to bury her in a very special place, the *Cave of the Two Chambers, known as Machpelah.*

Earlier in his travels, in Mamre, Abraham felt drawn to this cave surrounded by trees on a lovely piece of land. He walked into the cave and saw a great light. The light led Abraham through one of the cave's double chambers to what he recognized as the burial mound of Adam and Eve. He wanted to bury Sarah in this sacred cave.

The land was owned by a man named Ephron. Ephron offered the cave and land to Abraham as a gift. Instead, publically and in front of all their peoples, Abraham paid Ephron 400 shekels of silver for the land. The payment insured that the cave would be a resting place for Sarah, himself and their descendents. Abraham honored his wife Sarah by burying her in the Cave of Machpelah, near Mamre. Today the place is called Hebron or Al-Khalil.

On the day of Sarah's burial, there was a great procession.
All the people came to honor her life and mourn her death.

espondent after the loss of his mother, Isaac spent his time between the two places that offered him comfort—the Cave of Machpelah and Be'er L'chai Roi.

By now, Abraham was upset and concerned about his unhappy son. He felt Isaac needed something positive in his life. It was time to find him a wife. He called Eliezer, his trusted assistant, and asked him to go to the land of his birth family to find a wife for Isaac. Abraham and Eliezer both prayed that the journey would be successful.

With camels and silver and gifts for the bride-to-be, Eliezer set off for Haran, back to the land between two rivers. After days of traveling, he arrived at Haran, the place they had all left many years before. It was late afternoon when Eliezer sat down near a well to wait for the women to come for the evening's water. A beautiful young maiden arrived carrying a jug. Eliezer asked her for a drink. She filled her cup and gave it to him, then she offered to fetch water for his camels. This happened just as God had predicted when Eliezer and Abraham prayed.

Eliezer knew at once, that God had brought him to the right place, and he had found the right maiden. *Her name was Rebecca.* Genesis 24:15

Eliezer presented Rebecca with silver bracelets and a gold nose ring. Her family gave their blessing for this union.

The next day, Eliezer, Rebecca and her servants began their return journey. After days of travel, they reached the area of *Be'er L'chai Roi.* As the sun eased into the horizon, Rebecca saw a man, bathed in light, standing near the well. "Who is that man?" she asked. Eliezer said it was Isaac. Rebecca was smitten. She covered her face with her veil, signifying her willingness to marry, and as she did, Rebecca lost her balance and slid off her camel.

Isaac looked up at that same moment and saw Rebecca. She was beautiful and for him, it was love at first sight.

With the blessing of Abraham and the entire tribe, Isaac and Rebecca married.
They settled in Sarah's tent near The *Well of The Living-One-Who-Sees-Me*.

Abraham lived contentedly for a long time, and at the grand age of *one hundred seventy-five years, he breathed his last breath on earth.*
GENESIS 25:7

When Ishmael learned of his father's death he returned to the land of Canaan. He came to honor the life of his great father, and to reconcile with his brother. Together and in peace, Ishmael and Isaac buried their father Abraham at The Cave of Machpelah, next to his beloved wife Sarah.

Together and in peace, they mourned the death of their father, the father of all the faithful, Abraham.

Isaac, the son of Sarah, often returned to The Well Of The Living-One-Who-Sees-Me. Just as in Abraham's time, a severe drought came to the land. God told Isaac not to cross into Egypt. *God would protect Isaac and provide him with a bountiful harvest.* Genesis 26:2

Isaac trusted that God's underground aquifers would never stop flowing. He demonstrated great faith in God by never quarreling over water. As his flocks grew in number, his nomadic neighbors were occasionally jealous of his good fortune and would question his right to a well. Isaac would not try to justify his claim. Peacefully, he would gather his flocks and move to a new site. There he would dig a new well for his family and flocks, always grateful to God for the living-waters where a dove often came to splash. Isaac kept God's sacred underground aquifers open to all people.

Isaac and Rebecca became the parents of twin sons, Jacob and Esau. Esau married Ishmael's daughter, Mahalath. Genesis 28:9. Jacob married Leah and Rachel.

Isaac and Rebecca lived long lives. When they died, they were buried next to Abraham and Sarah in the Cave of Machpelah. Jacob and his wife Leah were also buried there.

n the Bible, Ishmael, son of Hagar, lived in an area close to Egypt where he became a great bowman. God assured Hagar that He would always "hear" her son.

At an early age, God granted Ishmael the skill of an archer. This gift held a hidden double message, formed in the shape of the bow. In the ancient Hebrew language the word for "bow" is "keshet" and the word for "rainbow" is the same, "keshet." Symbolically, Ishmael can lift his arched bow high, aim, and create a rainbow. From the earliest times dating back to Noah, the rainbow was a sign from God.

At the sign of the rainbow, a dove came to perch on the colors, signifying God's dream of peace for all of Abraham's family.

In Paran Hagar found Ishmael a wife. Ishmael's sons were named: Nebaioth, Kedar, Adbeel, Mibsam, Mishma, Dumah, Massa, Hadad, Tema, Jetur, Naphish, and Kedmah. GENESIS 25:12. His daughter was Mahalath, who married Esau.

It is said, that the Prophet Muhammad was born into the powerful Quraysh tribe, whose lineage decended from Kedar, second son of Ishmael more than 2500 years earlier.

In our *"double" retelling* of the stories of Abraham and his two sons, in the Bible, Isaac is offered up.

In the Islamic tradition, Ismail is the son to be sacrificed.
Regardless of the version, the inspiration is Abraham's willingness to follow the Voice of God.

Both sons fathered great nations.

Together the brothers, Abraham's sons,
complete the cycle of water and rainbow:
Isaac, pulling up God's blessing from the well below,
and Ishmael aiming high for a rainbow.

In the Muslim tradition, Ismael is known as the Father of the Arabs, the founder of the Quraysh tribal line which 2,500 years later would include Muhammad.

In the Judeo-Christian traditions Abraham and Isaac are known as Patriarchs.
Both Ismael and Isaac are Prophets in Islam.

In the Bible, God spoke to Abraham
This is my covenant with you, you shall be the father of a multitude of nations.

Genesis 17:4

In the Qur'an *"Salamun (peace) be upon Ibrahim!"*

Sura, 37:109

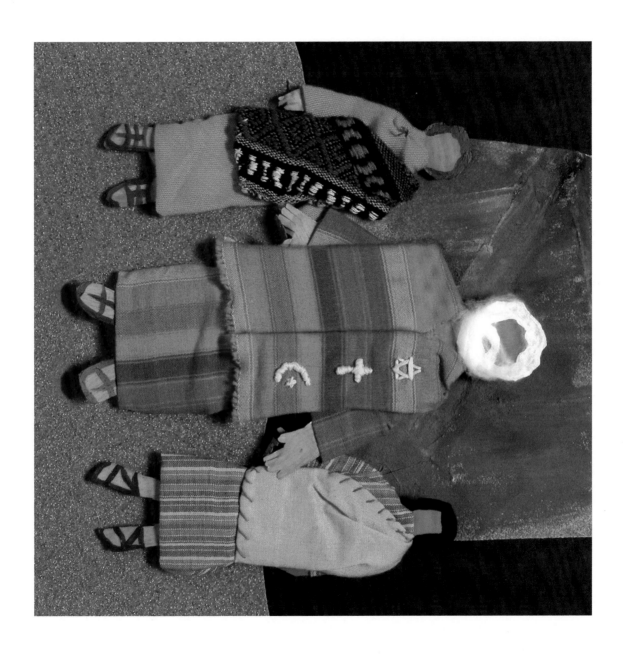

The Cave of Reconciliation

by Pecki Sherman Witonsky

For information regarding permission, write to:

DIAMOND ROCK PRESS
P.O. BOX 765
BRYN MAWR, PA 19010
www.cave*of*abraham.com
e-mail contact@cave*of*abraham.com

Library of Congress Cataloging–in–Publication Data
1. Biblical-Juvenile Literature
2. Quran-Juvenile Literature
3. Abraham-Juvenile Literature

ISBN: 0-9767766-0-X

Genealogy

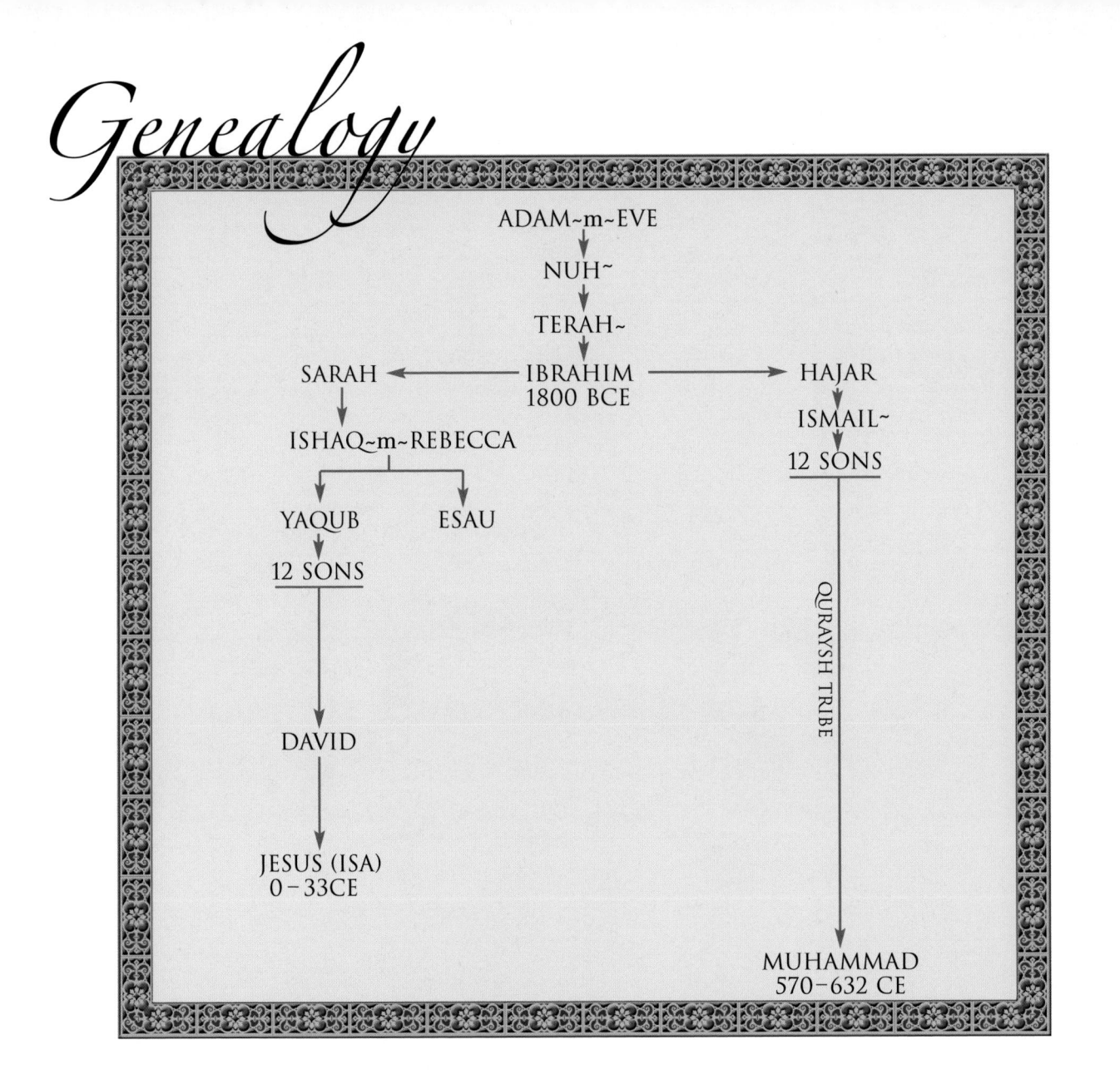

ADAM~m~EVE

NUH~

TERAH~

SARAH ← IBRAHIM → HAJAR
1800 BCE

ISHAQ~m~REBECCA

ISMAIL~

12 SONS

YAQUB   ESAU

12 SONS

QURAYSH TRIBE

DAVID

JESUS (ISA)
0–33CE

MUHAMMAD
570–632 CE

This is My covenant with you. You shall be the
father of a multitude of nations.

GENESIS 17:4

〰️

The book of the genealogy of Jesus Christ, the son of David,
the son of Abraham.

MATTHEW 1

〰️

Say, we believe in God, in what has been revealed to us
and what was revealed to Abraham, Ismail, and in the Books given
to Moses, Jesus, and the Prophets from their Sustainer. We make no
distinction between one and another.

SURA 2:136

〰️

These and these are the words of the living God.

TALMUD

These are stories about Ibrahim. Stories of Ibrahim's deep faith in Allah, God of Creation. Stories of his relationship with his two sons, Ismail and Ishaq, and their mothers, Hajar and Sarah.

These tales are ancient. They have been told by Muslims, Jews and Christians for generations - among families, as they sat around campfires and wellsprings, in the deserts long ago. Today, people of all three faiths continue to recount the stories in their holy places, in their homes and even in films.

At different times in history, depending on the teller, events and locations change. For example, in the Judeo-Christian account, Ishaq is offered up, while it is Ismail who is brought forth for sacrifice in the Islamic story. Regardless of the version, the inspiration is Ibrahim's willingness to follow the voice of God. In each story, God's life-giving underground waters spout up in deserts, separated by hundreds of miles, at different times. Whatever the time or the location, in all versions, God is the source, the Aquifer for all people of faith.

Whether Muslim, Jew, or Christian, at the heart of each telling is Ibrahim. Never faltering is the deep relationship between God and Ibrahim, and God, Ibrahim and all people of faith.

Here we retell stories, combining what we have heard, with what has been written in the Qur'an and the Traditions. If you turn this book around and start at the other side you will be able to read the stories of Abraham as told in the Bible.

As Muslims, Jews and Christians we are all descendents of Ibrahim, the father of our faiths. The father whose sons came together to peacefully bury him in the Cave of Machpelah. *A place whose destiny is Reconciliation.* The time has come for us to respect each other's faith in the One God, The Creator, Allah.

☾✵☽

Allahu'Akbar, Allahu'Akbar
God is the Greatest, God is the Greatest
Ash-hadu an – Laa'illaha Illal-laah
I bear witness that there is no deity worthy of worship except God
Ash-hadu anna Muhammad-an-Rusoulul Laah
I bear witness that Muhammad is the Messenger of God

ABOUT 600 C.E.

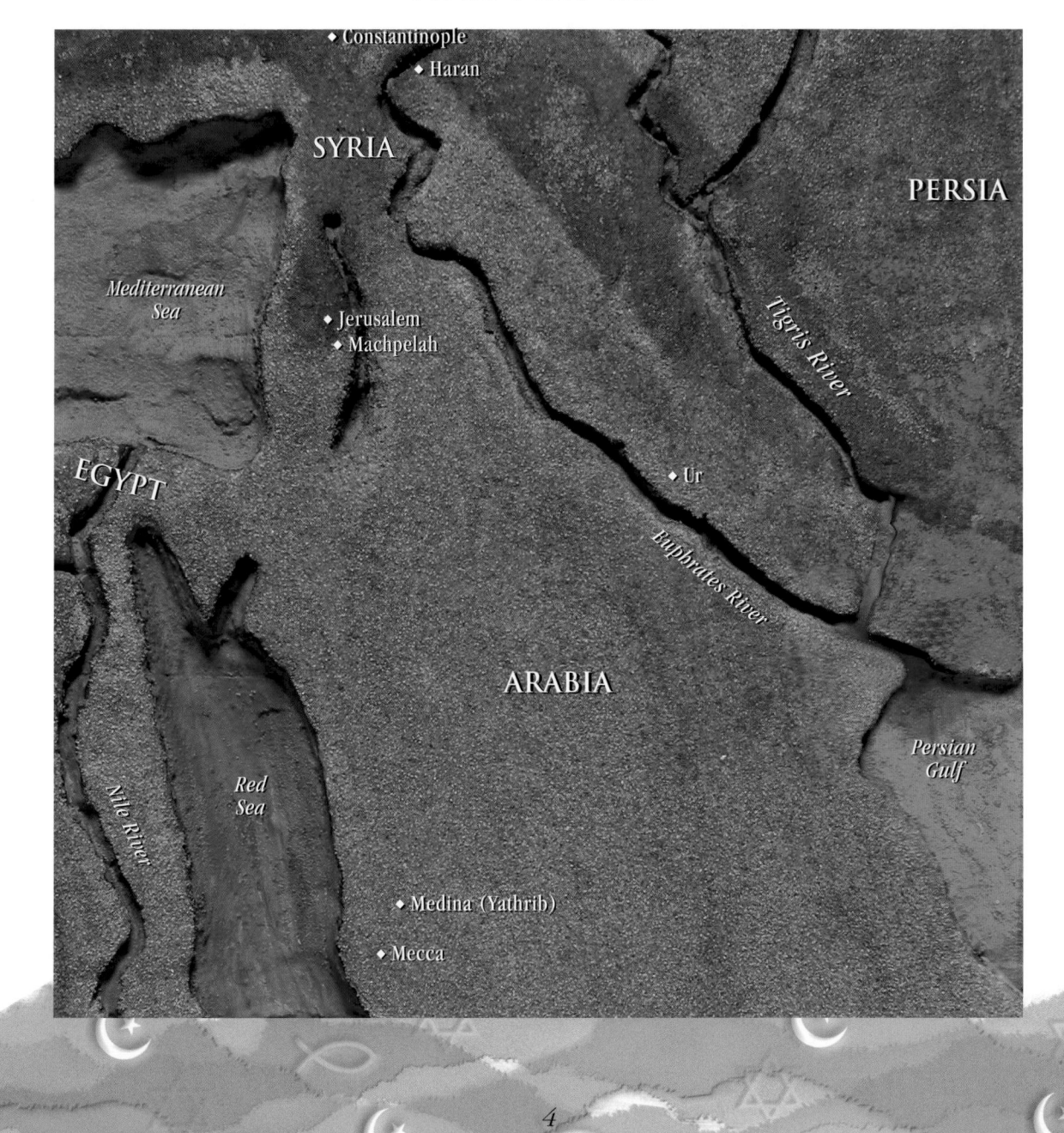

Constantinople

Haran

SYRIA

PERSIA

Mediterranean
Sea

Tigris River

Jerusalem

Machpelah

EGYPT

Ur

Euphrates River

ARABIA

Nile River

Red
Sea

Persian
Gulf

Medina (Yathrib)

Mecca

4

In 600 CE, Jews, Christians and Arabs lived in the city of Mecca (Makkah), in Arabia. Mecca was a growing city, an important hub where caravans from the South came loaded with spices to trade with caravans from the North laden with silk.

Every year Arab peoples came to Mecca from all directions on pilgrimage to honor 360 different tribal gods. God was understood to be the Creator and Sustainer of life, but was far removed from the daily needs. The local gods were called up to answer everyday needs and concerns.

Early in his life, Muhammad was respected as an honest man, a mediator and problem-solver. Muhammad and his friends, the merchants and caravan drivers shared their stories. Among the stories that were told were the Biblical tales of Abraham and the New Testament's stories about the life of Jesus.

One day Muhammad was meditating in a cave on a hillside when the Angel Gabriel appeared to him. The angel told him that God had a plan for him and the Arab people. Muhammad was to recite revelations from God. Faithfully for the next 22 years Muhammad recited these revelations. Muhammad spoke beautifully, so poetically about God that their hearts were opened and they gave up their idols and "surrendered" to the Will of Allah. The newly converted Muslims said, *There is no God but God (Allah) and Muhammad is the messenger of Allah.*

In Arabic the name for God is Allah.

In Muhammad's lifetime he was known and respected by his people in many roles. He was their religious, political and military leader and the greatest Prophet of the Islamic faith. God's revelations to Muhammad are written in the Qur'an, the Muslim holy book. The Jews and Christians who lived in Mecca were known as the "People of the Book."

In our story we retell the tales we have heard and read about Muhammad and Ibrahim.

In *Sura 17* there is a wonderful story about a great meeting that took place between Muhammad and Ibrahim on the seventh level of heaven. The Angel Gabriel came to Muhammad and instructed him saying, "*It is Allah's Will, mount the great white horse, Buraq, and journey to the farther temple* (in Jerusalem)." When there, Muhammad met Jesus and Moses. He then ascended a ladder and, on the seventh level of heaven, Muhammad met Ibrahim.

Muhammad and Ibrahim bonded instantly. Muhammad recognized Ibrahim as a "hanif." A hanif is one who believed in the One God, even before the time of the Jews and Christians. Therefore, Muslims believe that the Islamic faith is not a new faith, but one newly revealed and rooted in the life of Ibrahim, father of faith. SURA 3:67.

For the Christians, who were respected by Muslims as one of the "People of the Book" we read another heavenly story. In the New Testament in the Gospel of Luke we learn that Lazarus a God loving man, was near death. Lazarus was very poor, hungry and covered with sores. He begged crumbs from the table of a wealthy man and was rejected. Shortly thereafter Lazarus died and was lifted to heaven and welcomed by Abraham. Scripture tells us, *he was carried by angels into the bosom of Abraham.* LUKE 16:19-31.

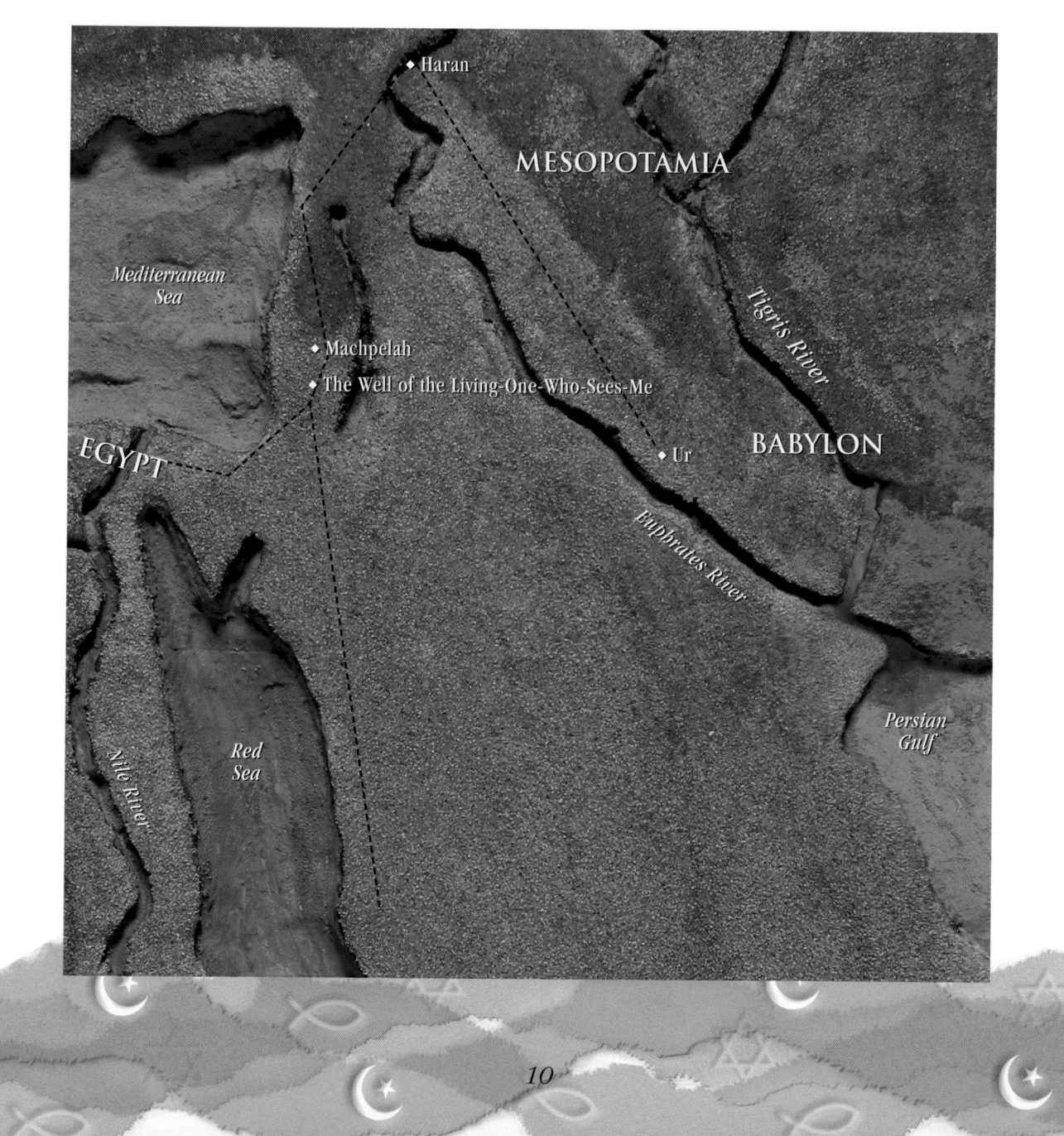

Haran

MESOPOTAMIA

Mediterranean
Sea

Tigris River

♦ Machpelah
♦ The Well of the Living-One-Who-Sees-Me

♦ Ur

BABYLON

EGYPT

Euphrates River

Persian
Gulf

Nile River

Red
Sea

**I**brahim heard a voice – the Voice of the Creator, the One God, filling his whole being with warmth and love. The Voice said, *Go forth to a land that I will show you, I will make you a great nation, you will be a blessing.* GENESIS 12:2.

Now another man might have been entirely perplexed. After all, Ibrahim was 75 years old, and he and Sarah were childless. But he realized that the Voice was the One he had been preparing for and waiting to hear his whole life. He knew it was the one Voice to trust and follow. He believed that, with the help of the Voice, the One God, that he and Sarah, could indeed become a great nation. As for his age, Ibrahim's father, Terah, was 70 when Ibrahim was born, and the Bible tells us Terah lived 205 years.

Again, and yet again, The Voice repeated *Go forth*. Ibrahim knew this didn't just mean go forth in the physical sense. It meant *go forth and go deeply within your heart*. It meant that Ibrahim was to follow the Voice with every ounce of his being, led and strengthened by a faith known by no other man. Somehow, Ibrahim knew that if he obeyed this awe-inspiring Voice, he would embark on a journey that would change his world forever.

Ibrahim had known of God since his early childhood.
He remembered an incident…

Ibrahim's father, Terah, made statues of gods. Today we call them "idols." These idols represented the different regional gods. Terah crafted these statues for the people and their king, Nimrud, who considered himself to be a god-king. The people prayed to Nimrud and the idols.

As a little boy Ibrahim played in his father's shop, among the statues. One day when he was alone in the shop, Ibrahim took a stick and smashed the idols. SURA 21:58 Then he put the stick in the hand of the largest statue.

When Terah saw the mess in the shop, he was enraged. "What happened?" he demanded. Pointing at the large statue, Ibrahim said, "He did it!" Terah responded, "That's impossible, these idols are not alive, they have no breath!"

"Then why do people pray to them?" asked Ibrahim.

Terah had no answer.

13

As Ibrahim grew into manhood, he told people his idea of the One Allah, the God of Creation.

King Nimrud was beginning to worry about the effect Ibrahim's stories had on some of the people, and he decided to stop him. Some of the people agreed with Nimrud and were afraid and cried *Build up a pyre and cast him into the blazing flames.* Sura 21:68 Nimrod had his slaves build a brick furnace filled with wood and ordered that Ibrahim be tied and placed inside. Nimrud himself started the fire to show the people he was the most powerful god-king.

But Allah, the God of Creation, sent an angel down to protect Ibrahim. Days later, when the slaves opened the grate to the furnace, Ibrahim walked out.

Nimrud never spoke of Ibrahim or Allah again.

**S**o when Ibrahim heard the Voice of God, he was ready to follow. After all, he had already questioned the idols and was saved from the furnace by an angel of God.

Go forth and go within. Leave where you are living, your father's family house.
Go to a place that I will show you. There I will make you a great nation.
GENESIS 12:1

When Ibrahim's wife Sarah saw the light in his eyes, she knew at once that it was time for them to leave their home in Haran. Still childless and advanced in years, Sarah did not understand how they could fulfill the "great nation" part of the promise. But as a devoted wife and faithful servant of God, she joined her husband willingly. She and Ibrahim believed that, if they kept faith in God, blessings would follow.

Sarah had the servants and slaves pack all their belongings, while Ibrahim and his chief steward Eliezer rounded up their flocks of animals. Together this small Ibrahamic clan departed from the rich, fertile land between the two rivers. They began their journey to a sparser place where the living waters would go underground to reappear in wells and cisterns.

Those faithful first steps thousands of years ago were the beginnings of a nation built to serve the One God, Allah. To this day those first steps still connect all believers in the One God.

Go forth and go within. Leave where you are living, your father's family house.
Go to a place that I will show you. There I will make you a great nation. GENESIS 12:1.

Ibrahim and Sarah journeyed to Shechem, where they found shade among the great trees. There, Ibrahim built an altar and dedicated it to God. Then they rested and watered their flocks. Ibrahim's step was light and confident, and Sarah was more beautiful than ever. Energized, they migrated south.

In time, Ibrahim and Sarah began to face great challenges. In the desert Negev they experienced a drought so severe that Ibrahim needed to temporarily move his tribe to Egypt.

At that time, Egypt was ruled by a Pharaoh, a man who proclaimed himself to be not only king, but also god of Egypt.

Pharaoh's guards were responsible for reporting all that went on in Egypt to him. They told Pharaoh that a new tribe had crossed onto his land and, among these people, there was a woman of exceptional beauty. The woman was Sarah.

Pharaoh visited the tribe of Ibrahim, and when he saw Sarah, he wanted her for himself. Now Sarah knew that it was illegal for a man—even a Pharaoh—to steal another man's wife, but they both knew that Pharaoh could order Ibrahim's death, then claim Sarah as his own. In order to save his own life, an anguished Ibrahim had Sarah pose as his sister.

Sarah was taken into Pharaoh's harem.

Pharaoh was intrigued by Ibrahim and spent time talking to him about worldly and godly matters. Pharaoh was so pleased with both "brother" and "sister" that he gave Ibrahim gifts of gold, silver, cattle and slaves. Among these gifts was a princess, whose name was Hajar.

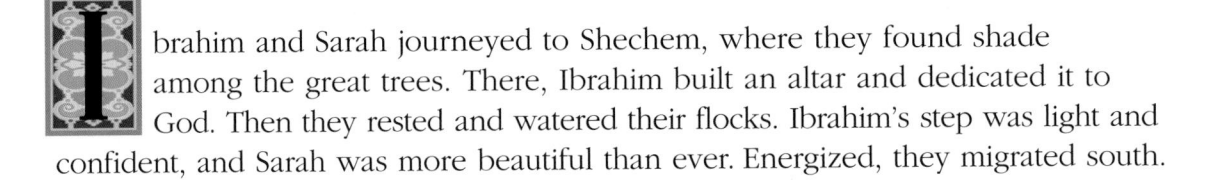

Sarah could not bear serving in Pharaoh's harem and she prayed to God for help. Seeing her anguish, God sent a plague on Pharaoh's house. When Pharaoh realized that Ibrahim and Sarah had tricked him, and that the God of Ibrahim had the power to bring a plague on his house, Pharaoh returned Sarah to Ibrahim and ordered them to leave Egypt.

Fearing Ibrahim's God, Pharaoh did not even take back the gifts.

When they left Egypt, Ibrahim gave Hajar to Sarah.

Ibrahim and Sarah had agreed to follow Allah's voice when He instructed Ibrahim to *Go forth to a place that I will show you.* As Sarah aged, she remained a great beauty, but her hopes of having a child were past. How could she help Ibrahim fulfill the promise that God had made to him early in their journey, in Shechem, at the great trees of Morah? There, God had told him *this land will belong to your children and your children's children's children forever.*

One night Sarah overheard a conversation her husband had with God. God reassured Ibrahim *Look up and count the stars, your descendants will number more than the stars. Only through your very seed will you have an heir.* GENESIS 15:4-5 Desperate to help, Sarah believed there was only one way to fulfill the promise. She would give Hajar to Ibrahim, as a second wife. Hajar went into Ibrahim's tent that one night, nervous, but filled with hope for the future.

Six weeks later Hajar and Sarah realized Hajar was pregnant with Ibrahim's child. As the months passed and Hajar's belly grew larger, she and Sarah quarreled frequently. Hajar ran away.

When she thought she could no longer survive, Allah sent an angel to her. At first, distressed and parched with thirst, Hajar did not see the angel standing before her. The angel asked, "Hajar where did you come from, and where are you going?" Hajar managed to tell her story. The angel showed Hajar a bubbling wellspring rising from Allah's underground aquifer. Hajar drank from the well and looked deeply at her own reflection. She realized that God had seen her, and she named the Well, *The Well of the Living-One-Who-Sees-Me.* GENESIS 16:13

Then the angel told Hajar of God's promise – that she would have a son, his name would be Ismail, and he would be the father of a great nation. The angel told Hajar to "*go back to Sarah and Ibrahim,*" GENESIS 16:9, so the promise would be fulfilled.

At the end of nine months, Hajar gave birth to a son. As Allah's angel had foretold, Ibrahim named him Ismail, *God Hears*.

By the Will of Allah, when Ibrahim was 99 years old he circumcised himself and every male in his tribe. Ismail was 13.

Allah instructed Ibrahim to take Hajar and Ismail south through barren deserts, where he would resettle them in a new land. They traveled for many days in a desolate valley. Ibrahim understood that he was to leave the two of them in this place between the two hills. Frightened, Hajar did not want to be left alone. Reassured by Ibrahim that it was the Will of Allah, Hajar said she understood, and they parted. Ibrahim prayed for Allah to save his family. Then he returned to Canaan. Sura 14:37.

Soon Hajar ran out of bread and water. Panicked, she ran between the two hills of As-Safa and Al-Marwa, looking for signs of grasses and water. She was very frightened and feared for their lives. Allah sent the angel Gabriel to Hajar. Gabriel pushed his heel into the sandy soil, and water gushed up. With great joy and gratitude to Allah, Hajar knew that they were saved.

Birds flying overhead saw the water and came to drink. Desert nomads traveling nearby saw the birds circling in the sky. They came to see. The water flowed freely and grasses began to grow. The people stayed, and a small community began to grow around Hajar and Ismail.

Today the city is called Mecca and water still flows freely from this sacred underground aquifer of God. The well is called *Zamzam*.

As he promised, Ibrahim visited Hajar and Ismail from time to time. On one of his trips, Ibrahim had a dream and realized that the message was from Allah. Sura. 37:102. He saw himself binding Ismail to an altar and sacrificing him. Troubled by this image, Ibrahim described his dream to Ismail who said, *Father if it is Allah's Will, do as you are commanded. I agree to surrender to Allah.* Sura 37:100-113. In sadness, but led by the Will of Allah, they trudged to a high place where Ibrahim built an altar and placed Ismail onto it.

Many times along the way, Satan beckoned to Ibrahim, posing as Allah telling him not to kill his son. But Ibrahim was not to be fooled by this impostor. He threw stones at Satan to keep him away, and to keep himself from believing in Satan's false promises. Ever faithful, Ibrahim was always able to distinguish between Satan and Allah.

When at last it was time for the slaying, Ismail said quietly, *Father, please do it quickly so you will not see my suffering. And allow me to remove my garment so that my mother will not see the blood.* Ibrahim took up his knife, closed his eyes and prepared to slay his son.

Before Ibrahim could bring his knife down, an angel of God grabbed his hand in mid-air and lowered it away from Ismail. Ibrahim managed to open his eyes. Relieved and stunned, he turned his anguished face away from his son and saw a ram struggling in the bushes. Ibrahim loosened Ismail and placed the ram on the altar.

Because both Ibrahim and Ismail were willing to surrender to Allah, they were rewarded. Ismail would become father of the Arabs.

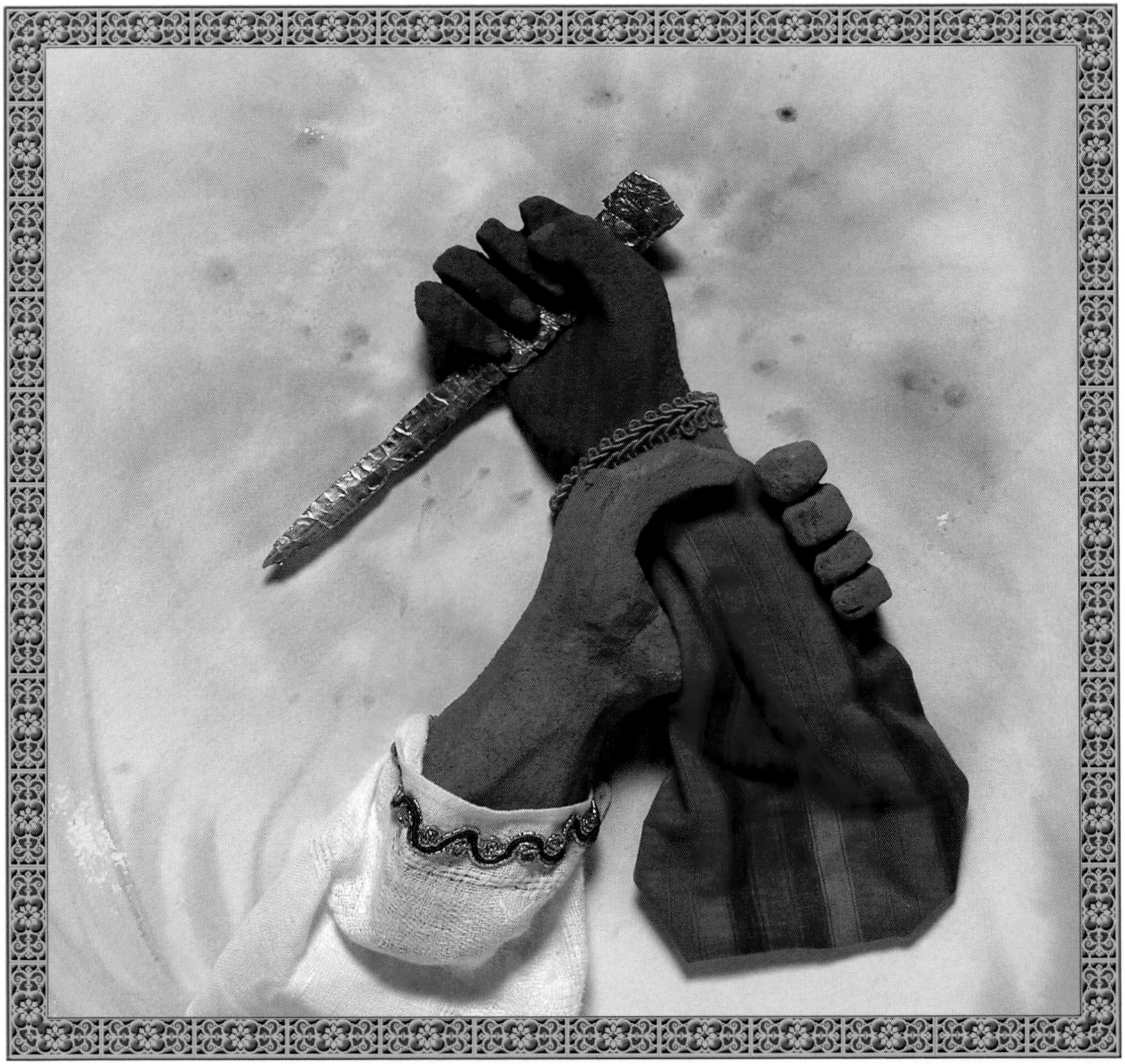

I brahim was told that Sarah, his first wife, would bear him a son whose name would be Ishaq (Isaac). Despite her advanced age, Sarah conceived and gave birth to Ishaq as Allah promised.

Praise be to Allah who has given me, in my old age Ismail and Ishaq! My Lord is indeed the Hearer of my prayer. SURA 14:39.

It is said, on anther visit to Hajar and Ismail, Ibrahim was guided by a breeze to a place not far from the Zamzam well. Ibrahim discovered that Adam had once built an altar to God on this sacred spot. Adam, the first man, had lived 20 generations before Ibrahim. It is said that Adam had seen the footprint of God on that site and had built an altar.

Ibrahim knew the altar was sacred. With Ismail's help, Ibrahim purified the site and rebuilt it stone by stone as an altar to Allah. The black stones were very heavy. In order for Ibrahim to place the top stones, Ismail gave him a stone to stand on.

It is said, Ibrahim's footprint was left on that stone. Ibrahim and Ismail prayed, *Oh Lord! Accept this service from us, for you are all-knowing and all-hearing!* SURA 2:125-7

Ibrahim called all the people and dedicated the sacred Holy House the great black shrine, the Ka'bah, a safe place for all people. The Ka'bah was to be used as a prayer house, a place of pilgrimage for all to visit, a place to bow and prostrate to God. SURA 14:37.

brahim lived contentedly for a long time, and at the grand age of one hundred seventy-five years, he breathed his last breath on earth.

When Ismail learned of his father's death he returned to the land of Ibrahim in Canaan. He came to honor the life of his great father, and to reconcile with his brother. Together and in peace, Ishaq and Ismail buried their father Ibrahim at The Cave of Machpelah, also known today as the Ibrahimi Mosque.

Together and in peace, they mourned the death of their father, the father of all the faithful, Ibrahim.

There is a story on the other side of this book that tells how Abraham was drawn to the cave and how he purchased the sacred burial place. The cave is located in the city of Hebron which is called Khalil Allah.

In Arabic it means the City-of-the-Friend-of-God.

shaq (Isaac), son of Sarah, often returned to The *Well Of The-Living-One-Who-Sees-Me*, the well where Hajar had first met an angel of God and learned that Ismail would become a great nation.

Ishaq trusted that God's underground aquifers would never stop flowing. He demonstrated great faith in God by never quarreling over water. As his flocks grew in number, his nomadic neighbors were occasionally jealous of his good fortune and would question his right to a well. Ishaq would not try to justify his claim. Peacefully he would gather his flocks and move to a new site. There he would dig a new well for his family and flocks, always grateful to God for the living-waters where a dove often came to splash. Ishaq kept God's sacred underground aquifers open to all people.

Ishaq and his wife Rebecca had twin sons, Yaqoub (Jacob) and Esau. Jaqoub married Leah and Rachel. Esau married Ismail's daughter, Mahalath.

Ishaq and Rebecca lived long lives. When they died they were buried next to Abraham and Sarah in the Cave of Machpelah. The Cave of Machpelah is also know as the Cave of the Patriarchs, or the Ibrahimi Mosque.

Ishaq became a great nation and is known as a prophet in Islam.

**I**smail, son of Hajar, lived in the area near Mecca. God promised Hajar that He would always "hear" her son. Ismail is known as a messenger of Allah, a Prophet.

At an early age, God granted Ismail the skill of archer. This gift had a double message, formed in the shape of a bow. In Arabic the word for "bow" and "rainbow" are the same—quas-qada(h). Symbolically, Ismail can lift his arched bow high, aim and invoke a rainbow. At the sign of a rainbow, a dove came to perch on the colors, signifying God's dream of peace for all of Ibrahim's family. In addition to his marksmanship, Ismail was known for his patience and good will.

Hajar found Ismail a wife. Ismail's sons were named: Nebaioth, Kedar, Adbeel, Mibsam, Mishma, Dumah, Massa, Hadad, Tema, Jetur, Naphish, and Kedmah. GENESIS 25:12

His daughter Mahalath, married Esau, one of Ishaq's sons.

Ismail lived 137 years.

It is said that the Prophet Muhammad was born into the powerful Quraysh tribe whose lineage is rooted in Kedar, second son of Ismail.

43

ntil the time of Muhammad, long after the time of Ibrahim and Ismail, the people forgot about God. However the tradition of a yearly pilgrimage to the Sacred Holy House – The Ka'bah – continued, and the people prayed to their local gods.

In 600 C.E., the great Prophet Muhammad cleansed and purified the city of Mecca of its idols. The sacred Ka'bah built by Ibrahim and Ismail was cleansed, rebuilt and rededicated to the One God, Allah.

Once a year at the time of pilgrimage, called the Hajj, millions of Muslims come to pray at the Ka'bah. Pilgrims circle the Holy Shrine seven times, counting from the place where Ibrahim left his footprint. In Arabic, the footprint of Ibrahim is called "Maqam Ibrahim." The Hajj is one of the five pillars of Islam. A ritual practice during the Hajj, or pilgrimage, is the ceremonial throwing of stones at Satan. This tradition honors Ibrahim's complete devotion to Allah and his unwillingness to be swayed by Satan.

Ibrahim's wife Hajar is remembered and honored when pilgrims run between the two hills of As-Safa and Al-Marwah seven times then drink from the healing waters from the well of Zamzam.

We believe in Allah,

and the revelation given to us,

and to Ibrahim, Ismail, Ishaq, Jacob, and the tribes,

and that given to Moses and Jesus,

and that given to (all) Prophets for their Lord:

We make no difference between one

and another of them

and we bow to Allah (In Islam).

SURA 2:136

45

The Cave has been recognized since Biblical times.

The layering of our religions

has added to the

authenticity of location and story.

It's destiny is as a

Cave of Reconciliation.

I n the Bible, in Genesis 23:16, we learn that the Cave was purchased by Abraham, as a burial place for his wife Sarah, himself and future generations. He bought the Cave and the surrounding land from Ephron the Hittite, for 400 shekels of silver. Historians think that Abraham may have lived about 1800 BCE.

For Jews

the Cave is called Me-arat Hamachpela. In Hebrew, it is called the Cave of the 'doubles or pairs' or the Cave of the 'tombs.' It is believed that Adam and Eve, Abraham and Sarah, Isaac and Rebecca, and Jacob and Leah, are buried there.

During the Roman Period

King Herod (2 BCE-39 CE) built a large structure over the Cave as a House of Prayer for the Jews.

Christians

built a Church over Herod's structure, during the time of the Crusades, (starting 1096 CE).

Muslim

Mamlukes conquered Hebron about 1300 CE and they built a Mosque on top of the crumbling site.

Today

Hebron is populated mostly by Muslim Palestinian Arabs. Muslims and Jews pray on site at the Cave. In Arabic, Hebron is known as Al-Khalil, the City of-the-friend-of-God. The Cave is also known as the Ibrahimi Mosque.

PRESENT DAY MAP OF THE REGION

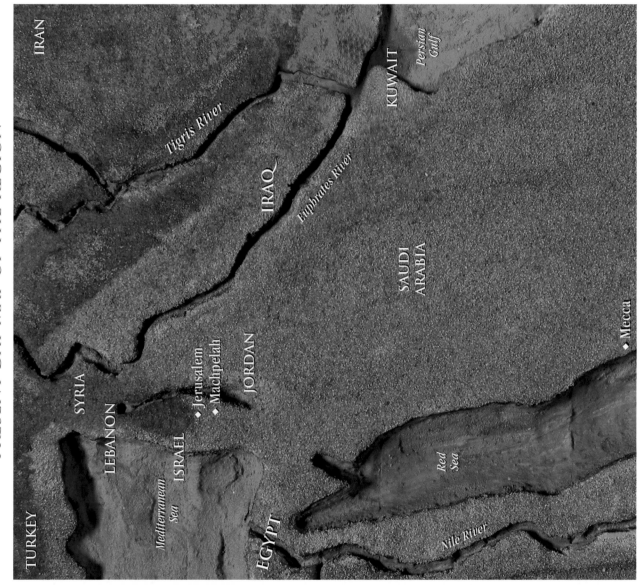

The Men of the Holy Books

Judaism	Christianity	Islam
Adam	Adam	Adam
Noah	Noah	Nuh
Abraham	Abraham	Ibrahim
Ishmael	Ishmael	Ismail
Isaac	Isaac	Ishaq
Jacob	Jacob	Yaqub
Joseph	Joseph	Yusuf
Moses	Moses	Musa
Aaron	Aaron	Harun
David	David	Dawud
Solomon	Solomon	Sulaiman
Ezekiel	Ezekiel	Dhuil-Kifl
Jonah	Jonah	Yunus
Zechariah	Zechariah	Zakariyya
	John	Yuhya
	Jesus	Isa
		Hud
		Shuaib
		Muhammad

As connectors and builders of our collective and unique beliefs in The One God. These individuals are honored in diverse ways because of the different roles they played in the unfolding story.

In Islam these men are called Prophets.